I0164409

PROTOCOL

*How the Character of our President's Reflects
Our Political & Spiritual Climate.*

(Jeremiah Letters Volume 2)

By
Christopher Gore

© Copyright 2019 Christopher Gore

New King James Version (NKJV)
Scripture taken from the New King James Version®. Copyright © 1982 by Thomas Nelson. Used by permission. All rights reserved.

Amplified Bible (AMP)
Copyright © 2015 by The Lockman Foundation, La Habra, CA 90631. All rights reserved.

All rights reserved. This book is protected by the copyright laws of the United States of America. This book may not be copied or reprinted for commercial gain or profit. The use of short quotation or occasional page copying for personal or group study is permitted and encouraged. Permission will be granted upon request for all other uses. Otherwise, no part of this publication may be reproduced, distributed, or transmitted in any form or by any means, including photocopying, recording, or other electronic or mechanical methods, without the prior written permission of the publisher, except in the case of brief quotations embodied in critical reviews and certain other noncommercial uses permitted by copyright law.

While the author has made every effort to provide accurate internet addresses at the time of publication, neither the publisher nor the author assumes any responsibility for errors or for changes that occur after publication. Further, the publisher does not have any control over and does not assume any responsibility for author or third-party websites or their content.

Contact the Author

Light Bearer Publishing Company
Attn: Reverend Christopher A. Gore
579 Groundhog Lane; Smyrna, DE 19977
christophergore@lighthousechurchinc.org

Previous works:
What Now??!!: Moving Past the Election of 2016
(The Jeremiah Letters) (Volume 1)
ISBN #: 978-0-9861572-8-8

ISBN #: 978-0-9861572-7-1

For Worldwide Distribution, Printed in the U.S.A.

Acknowledgments:

Giving honor unto my Lord and Savior Jesus Christ; who has endued me with the knowledge and strength to finish this project for His glory.

…To my lovely wife; Kathryn: your love, your help, and your support has encouraged me to step further into this realm. Thanks for the wonderful cover design.

…To my mother & father; I owe you both everything. If it weren't for your mentorship, guidance, grace, & love, nothing I do would ever be accomplished. Mom, thank you for your friendship, strength, Bible knowledge, but most of all your love. Dad, you see me and you are in that cloud of witnesses. I love and miss you.

…To my pastor; mentor and friend; Rev. Barbara Lynch: for encouraging me to serve our Heavenly Father with all my heart.

…To my longtime friend; Mark Johnson: for driving me and a group of aspiring artists to a Church creative arts competition and for being the critical eye that I needed to fine tune this book.

…Unto everyone else who stood on the sidelines cheering me on…

I release to you my heartfelt gratitude!

Edited by:

Kathryn R. Gore, Patricia 'Pattie' Hinchey, & Mark Johnson

Dedicated with love unto…

My Father – Cephus L. Gore

My Grandparents – Cephus V. & Mary L. Gore;
& Allen Y. & Ruby L. Jones

My Uncle – Allen Jones Jr.

My Friend – Tina Harris

My Friend – Lawrence Lynch

…my "great cloud of witnesses".

Hebrews 12: 1 (AMP)
Therefore, since we are surrounded by so great a
cloud of witnesses [who by faith have testified to the
truth of God's absolute faithfulness], stripping off
every unnecessary weight and the sin which so easily
and cleverly entangles us, let us run with endurance
and active persistence the race that is set before us,

TABLE OF CONTENTS

Foreword

I appreciate the straightforward way Rev. Christopher Gore has written his new book "Protocol".

This timely book is very essential for today and very informative as to what is taking place in the Government.

He takes us through the steps to what has been transpiring in the Government to undermine the teachings in God's Word - The Holy Bible and what the Church's responsibility is today to bring God back into our Government.

I have known Rev. Gore for many years and appreciate him as a friend and for his deep interest and passion for the welfare of our Government. God has gifted him to understand the function of the Government and he uses this gifting very wisely.

I pray as you read this insightful new book you will understand everything God would have you receive.

By Pastor/Evangelist Barbara Lynch

Preface:

Let every soul be subject to the governing authorities. For there is no authority except from God, and the authorities that exist are appointed by God. **Romans 13: 1 (NKJV)**

The Church in this nation has a responsibility to demonstrate the truth of God's Word to the people of this nation. The Church cannot shirk responsibility because it is inconvenient.

At all costs the Church must pay the price to show the world who our God is.

Rev. Christopher Gore

Introduction

Seasons Change

This nation has been under a period of judgment because the Church has not yet cleaned up its ways before the Lord. There is a remnant of people within the Church who have been crying out before God for change but an overwhelming majority are still practicing sin.

Everything in life has its cycles and seasons. The political system of this nation is no different. In one moment things can change drastically. We have seen the ideology of our nation shift from good to bad and then back in a matter of what seems likes seconds. There are periods where this change is as violent as a hurricane or as peaceful as a babbling brook. Change is here, ready or not!

The Bible gives clear instruction to those who read it. The instruction is wrought with directives that mandate us to honor those in authority over us. It even gives instructions for how slaves should treat their masters. Bottom line was respect for authority. The people of our nation have walked away from this practice of respecting authority. There used to be a general respect for authority, but sin has abounded and the foundations of our nation have eroded.

This shift away from respect for authority is leading the people of this nation towards total rebellion. The shift that has occurred in the thinking of people in general has brought the United States closer to anarchy than can ever be imagined. Those who thrive on evil seek to use this shift to their advantage. The remnant church must be aware that this shift has its roots in rebellion against authority. Just like satan rebelled and was eventually separated from God, man in his own way is rebelling and drawing himself away from God by resisting the authority that has been set over us. Whether you like it or not all authority is from God.

What about the case where that authority is unjust, inhumane, or ungodly? Did that authority come from God? The hard answer is yes, it did. The reason this authority came from God is very simple. God uses authority to correct. There are many cases in the Bible where Israel rebelled, and God placed/allowed an unrighteous king to gain authority over them. This nation is no different. We fell into the same error as they did and because of this the citizens of this nation reaped what was sown. In the 2008 elections the Church allowed itself to be silenced and a grave abomination took place; that abomination became the "Obama" nation.

The negligence of the leaders of the Church of America was a direct influence on why the people of this nation chose Barack Obama as President. Former President Obama was not chosen based upon what God wanted for this nation. He was chosen by the citizens of this Nation who did not have the guiding voice of the Church who was willing to engage in politics. Many in the Church of America refused to participate in the elections because the leaders of the Church took an anti-politics stance.

In a 2004 piece, Christianity Today dubbed Lucado "America's Pastor," alluding to his broad appeal to mainstream Americans. Part of that appeal can be attributed to his approach to politics: typically, he stays out of it. He never endorsed or opposed a presidential candidate. [i]

This refusal from Church leaders to take a stance has the nation reeling from the aftermath of what was done.

One of the most damaging things that occurred was the disrespect and dishonoring of authority. This disrespect and dishonoring came through two sources: one, the Church and second, the former President of the United States, Barack Obama. After the 2008 election many Christian leaders unknowingly practiced rebellion because they did not honor the authority that came through the Office of the President. This "joke" started going around the Church.

Psalms 109:8 says, 'Let his days be few; and let another take his office.' The citation is being passed around the Internet as a rallying cry against President Obama. [ii]

It was a passive-aggressive way of expressing disrespect to the President. This joke made its way around churches in this nation and became very popular. This joke showed that there was no recognition that God had placed Obama in office to judge the Church for its previous years of sin.

Not only did the Church not honor that authority but they taught their followers to do the same. They refused to pray for the President. This became rebellion. This rebellion began a cycle of disrespect towards the authority that God had placed over us as a nation. Some even went so far as to call him different names. This fostered the attitude that prevails today in 2019, the attitude of *"That's Not My President".*

"That's not my President…" was started by the Church. The Church would not allow God to use them to speak to the issues of the day because of passivity and as a result it lost its ability to influence this nation. This caused the gates of this nation to be opened to rebellion. The blatant disrespect for authority was permitted by God but it revealed its consequences.

This open door of rebellion by the Church has caused many to distrust the message from the Church. This distrust has caused many who were on their way into the Kingdom of God to turn around and walk back out the door. There has been confusion and miscommunication from the Church.

Let me explain what I mean. Because the Church stood in between the two opinions of 1) doing what was right and 2) honoring the President (Obama at the time), this opened the door for confusion to take place in the Church. The confusion came as a result of leaders in the Church making the choice to not do what was right in the sight of God. For the Church that was a full acknowledgment that God was judging this nation for its immoral behavior in its leaders, because the Church would not stand in holiness and righteousness and then proclaim that in the land. We have the mess that we have today because of this.

There is such a fear of telling the truth by the Church that we have giving up our right to stand in the place that God has called us to. We are called to judge between right and wrong. Our failure to take on this responsibility has brought about the indecision. The indecision comes from the Church not having a single voice. There are liberals versus conservatives within the Church. Both have their good points, but both have their bad points.

The Church should neither have a liberal voice or conservative voice. The voice coming out of the Church should just be God's voice. The Church should only represent God. If God's angry that should be communicated from the Church. If God's happy that should be communicated from the Church. The Church is miscommunicating because we are not speaking what God would speak because we are not doing what God would do because our ways are no longer His ways.

This has caused division to take place. The enemy is using this division to defeat us. This division is causing an indistinct sound to come out of the Church. This indistinct sound has been deadly not only to the Body of Christ but to the world as well. Disunity kept the Church from bringing the clarity that this nation needed to effect change within our borders, and this has caused us to reap what we have sowed. This reaping has affected every area of this nation.

There are those who prayed for Obama as unto the Lord and God honored those prayers but there were far more who disobeyed God and because of this they did not earn God's trust and the trust of the people. This has stirred rebellion in the hearts of God's people, and they sowed that rebellion into this nation via their families. We see this rebellion trickle down from the home out in the community.

The seeds of disrespect for authority started in the home. The husband disrespects and dishonors his wife. The wife disrespects and dishonors the husband. Our children grow up in an environment where they live and see disrespect and they grow up in environments where there is no love for authority. What they see their parents do to each other is then carried out into society. Children mimic the behavior that they see in the home and the disdain that they have for authority is further reinforced by the enemy who thrives on rebellion.

There was a time where just for the sake of the position, people respected authority. It was protocol. It was the right thing to do. That does not mean that all who walked in authority were right but just because they carried that authority it was respected. There was no questioning that authority. It was just respected. This book will focus in on what has happened to the authority structure in this Nation.

We will take a journey and see how this disrespect has caused the highest office in this land to become polluted with disrespect and dishonor. It will highlight how the seasons have changed. If the Church humbles itself, our culture can reposition and shift back into its godly origination and once again be a voice for God and communicate His thoughts to the world and the Church.

Selah

[i] https://www.christianitytoday.com/ct/2016/february-web-only/why-max-lucado-broke-his-political-silence-for-trump.html
[ii] https://www.csmonitor.com/USA/Politics/2009/1116/biblical-anti-obama-slogan-use-of-psalm-1098-funny-or-sinister

An Abomination That Causes Desolation
Chapter 1
Tracing the Disintegration of
Spiritual Authority in This Nation

³¹ And forces shall be mustered by him, and they shall defile the sanctuary fortress; then they shall take away the daily *sacrifices,* and place *there* the abomination of desolation.

³⁶ "Then the king shall do according to his own will: he shall exalt and magnify himself above every god, shall speak blasphemies against the God of gods, and shall prosper till the wrath has been accomplished; for what has been determined shall be done. ³⁷ He shall regard neither the God of his fathers nor the desire of women, nor regard any god; for he shall exalt himself above them all. ³⁸ But in their place he shall honor a god of fortresses; and a god which his fathers did not know he shall honor with gold and silver, with precious stones and pleasant things.

Daniel 11: 31, 36 – 38 (NKJV)

On the surface this scripture is about a real man, the antichrist who will come on the scene and fulfill prophecy but on another level the antichrist spirit has been prevailing in the world ever since Jesus died on the cross. However, with each passing stage as we draw closer to the time of the end there will be a people who will seek to set the world up to receive the real antichrist. They will walk in his demonic anointing and atmosphere and prepare the rest of the world to receive him. This really is a mocking of the anointing, but it will take place according to the Bible.

The antichrist spirit has opened the doorway to any and everything that is unclean. This spirit has manifested uncleanness in all forms. When it invades the Holy Place it will bring desolation to the earth. This abomination that causes desolation is unholy and unrighteous. Abomination means a thing or action that is vile, vicious or terrible. Daniel was shown a vision of an actual being coming into the Temple fortress and causing it to become defiled. At this point in Daniels vision, the Presence of God must not be abiding in the Temple fortress. For a purpose, yet to be revealed, this evil will be allowed to enter the Temple and defile it. Under normal conditions nothing unclean would ever be allowed to enter the Temple. Yet Daniel had a vision of this event taking place so clearly that it could not be denied.

Bible history teaches that when the priests were unclean and went before God in such a state they were struck down by God's glory. The sacredness of the Temple fortress being violated by this impurity will signal to Israel the beginning of a chain of events that will bring about swift and sudden destruction. The nature of this destruction will cause a stir in the natural realm. It will mark the destruction of natural authority. God's faithfulness will prevail and His covenant with Abraham shall be fulfilled according to God's plan.

The leaders in our nation have allowed for abominations of various sorts to take place in the highest offices of our nation. Many of our leaders are openly homosexual, many have criminal records, and many more lead lifestyles that are not biblical in nature. Up until recently there was a strong sense of shame that kept these practices in the closet. Today these abominations are done openly for the public to see. There is no longer a sense of shame for participating in these deviant acts.

It does not stop there because those who commit these abominations are not content to participate in these acts alone. They now have to make sure that they convince others to join in to what they are doing. They are not content with just being deviant themselves they are seeking to bring other people into their deviancy. These leaders are causing open doors in the Spirit realm. These open doors to sin in the natural realm causes the heavens to be closed over us. These closed heavens open the way for our nation to be judged.

"Gross Darkness" has taken root in our land. Julian Assange, the founder of Wiki Leaks, revealed that members of the Clinton team were practicing pedophilia (sexual exploitation of children) and witchcraft. Let's read what he found.

> "There is hard evidence that Bill Clinton traveled at least 26 times (sometimes without his bodyguards, it is all in the pilot logs) to billionaire and convicted pedophile Jeffrey Epstein's Island on board his plane, dubbed the "Lolita Express," as it is in this plane that the guests could allegedly have sex with minors. With this in mind, it is disturbing to notice that other Podesta emails refer to children as being the "entertainment" at pool parties almost entirely attended by middle-aged men involved in politics."[iii]

> "One of the initial disturbing finds in this collaborative investigation was the "art performance" of "Spirit Cooking," that has been enjoyed by the Podestas, Alefantis, and even the Clintons. "Spirit Cooking" is the performance of the witch, Marina Abramovic, and is "inspired" by occult sacrament ritual stemming from

Aleister Crowley's Enochian-inspired doctrine of Thelema, which has been loosely categorized as "sex magick," which is often coupled with traditional Tantra in certain senses."[iv]

These witchcraft practices listed in the Wiki Leaks documents show evidence of evil acts that have been occurring for quite some time by some well know and not so well-known heads of state. The ugly truth is that many different types of abominations have been occurring. There has been a lack of godliness and purity by our political and spiritual leaders.

As we look at ourselves in contrast to some of the things Israel has done, a terrible thing is going on within this nation, that is rebellion against authority. Like never before we are seeing a growing disrespect for authority. This disrespect is being birthed in reverse. It is not coming from the bottom upward but it is being birthed from the top down. The enemy has planted his members in various positions throughout our government. These members walk in some of the vilest and twisted ways of thinking imaginable. It is hard to believe that this level of evil could exist on such a scale but it does.

We must mature and think in the Spirit. We must stop thinking the way that we do and realize that the enemy has an agenda that he is working to complete. This agenda involves taking down the inner framework and fundamental truths in which our nation was built upon. The principle of respect for authority is one of those fundamental truths. The agenda that is being used to take down this Nation includes creating an atmosphere where authority is disrespected. Many people do not comprehend how respect for authority plays a role in the stability of our nation.

There are two concepts that Jesus followed in the area of authority that will be helpful to understand what is really happening. Concept one, Jesus' Kingdom was not of this world. Concept two, Jesus practiced respect for authority.

> ³⁵ Pilate answered, "I am not a Jew, am I? Your own people and their chief priests have handed You over to me. What have You done [that is worthy of death]?" ³⁶ Jesus replied, "My kingdom is not of this world [nor does it have its origin in this world]. If My kingdom were of this world, My servants would be fighting [hard] to keep Me from being handed over to the Jews; but as it is, My kingdom is not of this world."
>
> **John 18: 35 - 36 (AMP)**

Concept one, there is a misconception among Christians that Jesus' Kingdom is of this world. It is not. Any kingdom that comes from this world will be filled with darkness and will be subject to corruption. In God, there is no darkness, no corruption, and no violation of the fruit of the Spirit. But in this world all of those defilements exists and are manifested. They occur because inherent in man is a sin nature that cannot be redeemed outside of Christ and scripture is clear that those who belong to God live in the Spirit. It is with this knowledge and understanding that you can properly apply what Jesus also taught about the Kingdoms of this world

> ¹³ Then they sent some of the Pharisees and Herodians to Jesus in order to trap Him into *making* a statement [that they could use against Him]. ¹⁴ They came and said to Him, "Teacher, we know that You are truthful and have no personal bias toward anyone; for You are not influenced by outward appearances *or* social status, but in truth You teach the way of God. Is it lawful [according to Jewish law and tradition] to pay the poll-tax to [Tiberius] Caesar, or not? ¹⁵ Should we pay [the tax] or should we not pay?" But knowing their hypocrisy, He asked them, "Why are you testing Me? Bring Me a coin (denarius) to look at."¹⁶ So they brought one. Then He asked them, "Whose image and inscription is

this?" They said to Him, "Caesar's." [17] Jesus said to them, "Pay to Caesar the things that are Caesar's, and to God the things that are God's." And they were greatly amazed at Him.

Mark 12: 13 – 17 (AMP)

Concept two was the practice of respect for authority. Jesus respected authority. Jesus knew that all authority came from the Father. With this understanding you can see how far the Church and the world has fallen away from God. Understanding where the Church is now is the key to discerning the spiritual atmosphere in this season. There is such a rebellion in the Church towards God that it is hard for the Church to demonstrate proper respect for authority. This is sin. Sin brings darkness. So if you understand and properly apply these two concepts you will have a healthy perspective of authority.

As a believer you cannot pretend that darkness does not exist. Failure to comprehend darkness is a failure of understanding your role in dispelling darkness. If you don't believe darkness exists how can you be in agreement with Christ and war against darkness? You should be so full of light that an automatic separation comes between you and darkness.

We do have leaders in our political and church realms of our nation that walk in darkness. Because of this, they have a negative influence over this nation. The founding leaders of our country in the beginning lived by the morals and principles found in the Bible and because of it this nation prospered. The leaders honored God and God blessed us because of it. The leaders had a covenant that they followed but over time they have stopped honoring that covenant. Like, Israel, we are subject to similar penalties from God when our leaders go astray.

When it comes to our nation and its leaders we are held to a higher standard by God. What we do in the natural affects us spiritually. If our leaders normalize a behavior that is deemed unholy by God they arouse God's wrath. The normalization of bad behaviors in our leaders is causing sin to be passed down from generation to generation. Normalization of something does not mean that it is approved by God. It just means people have become desensitized to the real effects of that behavior. Normalization of sin causes God to move away from us. The more something becomes normalized the less shocked people are by the sin. The less shocked people are by sin the easier it is for lines of decency to be erased.

> Righteousness [moral and spiritual integrity and virtuous character] exalts a nation, but sin is a disgrace to any people.
> **Proverbs 14: 34 (AMP)**

Our society has come a long way technologically but spiritually we have in fact regressed. The technological advances did not bring with it an automatic increase in our ability to reason and equate bad behavior with bad consequences. Former Secretary of State, Hillary Clinton committed many acts of treason by using a personal server to store government emails. Some of these emails were classified in nature and should have only been viewed through secured processes. This appears to be an act of treason and put many lives at risk. Hillary was exonerated by the Obama Justice Department. Anyone else under similar circumstances would have been made to stand trial.

Recently the television actor, Jussie Smollet whom faked a hate crime against himself. It was discovered by the State of Illinois and the State of Illinois placed 16 felony charges against him for faking a hate crime, Smollet was arrested and is awaiting trial while he remains free on bail. Somehow the Prosecutor for the State of Illinois dropped all 16 counts against him with no explanation given. It appears, there is concrete evidence against him but there are many speculations that his friends in the Democratic Party are the reason he was not made to stand and give an account for his actions. Righteousness exalts a nation, but we do not have righteousness we have lawlessness.

The clear line of right and wrong is being extinguished. Our political leaders are an example of this phenomenon. When you look down through the years at the Office of the President there were some Presidents who had moral failures. No one is perfect and it would be foolish to place this expectation of perfection upon any of the Presidents who serve this Nation.

The Bible says that all have sinned and have fallen short of the Glory of God. Our 29th President, Warren Harding had extra-marital affairs and fathered a child during one of those affairs. Our 35th President John F. Kennedy was reportedly known to be a womanizer and had an affair with actress Marilyn Monroe. Our 36th President Lyndon B. Johnson claimed to have more women than President Kennedy. Whether Johnsons claim was verified is not the issue, Johnson wanted to portray himself as a person with a womanizing persona.

In more recent years, our 42nd President, William Jefferson Clinton, an Evangelical Christian believed in God and the Bible but throughout his entire career as a politician. It was reported that he has had one sex scandal after another. This was heavily detailed in Special Prosecutor Ken Stars Report in 1998. The sex scandal claims escalated during his Presidency with a scandal involving the intern, Monica Lewinsky after she was found to have given Clinton oral sex on several occasions in the White House.

Many conversations were took place from the pulpit, the streets, back room parlors, and the world of academia. These conversations were typical but what was atypical was the media coverage glorifying President Clinton as a hero because of his indiscretions. President Clinton's behaviors helped contribute to the normalization of oral sex among teens and young adults in America.

The first teen studies for oral sex were done in 2002. Former President Clinton served in office from January 20, 1993 – January 20, 2001. Even with the outbreak of A.I.D.S. in the 80's one doesn't find evidence of such an outward participation of oral sex but the practice of oral sex grew after Clinton's Monica Lewinsky scandal. They never had a reason to do such studies on this subject but oral sex was unheard of but now look at what has occurred. Now, look at what was found.

> Oral sex among all teens: Among teens ages 15 to 19, a similar percentage of males and females engaged in oral sex (55 percent of males and 54 percent of females). Older teens were more likely to engage in oral sex. Specifically, among teens ages 18 to 19, 70 percent of males and 72 percent of females reported having ever engaged in oral sex, compared with 44 percent of males and 42 percent of females ages 15 to 17.[v]

> For young adults, 87 percent of females ages 20 to 24 said they had vaginal intercourse, while 85 percent said they had oral sex. By age 20-24 years, 85 percent of males had vaginal intercourse and 82 percent had any oral sex.[vi]

The normalization of oral sex was a door that was opened by then President Clinton. The Church was already wavering in convictions. Church leaders refused to talk about oral sex behind the pulpit and among many others who supported the practice amongst their married and unmarried members.

Top evangelical leaders were trying to gain political favor or keep the offering monies coming into their church so the matter was not addressed with clarity. Very few would call what President Clinton did wrong on the false grounds of separation of Church and State. Many Church leaders would not address politics at all and the ones who did were instantly slapped with the label of being "judgmental".

The long term effects of what took place are still being seen in this nation today. The people who lived through that era began to see the Office of the President through a different set of eyes. It is not a surprise anymore that moral failures occur with leaders in every office and institution in our nation. What is a surprise is how these moral failures are dealt with. If you are a member of one political party over the other a moral failure may cause you to lose your office or keep it dependent upon where your chair is seated in the political spectrum. What's even more absurd is that if you are a part of certain party the levels to which you can get away with pure evil are reaching unprecedented levels.

We live in a much smaller world today. Assuming you can hide these types of incidents is tantamount to not living in reality. In some cases, these failures were covered up by the media. In other cases they were reported and called out for what they were. Bad behavior by someone who is a leader should be taken seriously as leaders are held to a higher standard.

With President Clinton's oral sex scandals, this signaled a downgrading of the Presidential Office because people lost respect not only for him as a person but for the Office of the President in general.

However, you want to dissect these events you have to look at two factors. Factor one, the morals of society have changed: Divorce is more acceptable, cheating on your spouse is more acceptable, even abandoning your family is acceptable. Factor two, the loss of moral light in the Church has kept the Church from being able to properly intercede for this nation.

The unintended outcome is that society in general has no expectation that leaders will live moral lives. So many failures and breaches of trust have occurred that it is no longer a shock when a leader confesses some moral failure. This is not the issue. The issue is that at present we are as a society living at a lower standard and these lower standards are being passed into the next generation. This next generation will continue the trend downward, and away from living a moral standard at all.

This moves us to the "Everybody is Doing it Fallacy". This is a fallacy that states that since "Everyone is living foul or because they are not living a good moral life, I have the freedom to do the same. I don't have to live right and in turn I do not have to submit to an authority figure or higher power. When you have this level of breakdown within the structure of any governing body, this is an open door for the formation of anarchy and rebellion.

The mindset persists within our society that if one can find fault with authority that gives one a pass from following any rules. One does not have to obey the laws of this land because the leaders themselves are not doing the same. We have had years of steady, repeated breakdowns in our society in this area of leadership and it is causing a toll that few understand at this given time. This is just now starting to be understood and seen for what it is. We have an open door looming for a spirit of lawlessness to abound.

> [11] Many false prophets will appear and mislead many.
> [12] Because lawlessness is increased, the love of most people will grow cold.
>
> **Matthew 24: 11 – 12 (AMP)**

> ⁷ For the mystery of lawlessness [rebellion against divine authority and the coming reign of lawlessness] is already at work; [but it is restrained] only until he who now restrains it is taken out of the way. ⁸ Then the lawless one [the Antichrist] will be revealed and the Lord Jesus will slay him with the breath of His mouth and bring him to an end by the appearance of His coming.
>
> **2 Thessalonians 2: 7 – 8 (AMP)**

The mystery of lawlessness as quoted in 2 Thessalonians above is rebellion against divine authority. My earlier premise in the introduction is directly from Romans 13: 1. "All authority comes from God..." One must reflect on this truth and complete the path to see how divine law inspires natural law. Anyone who has studied different cultures throughout history can testify of the truth that many natural laws have been birthed from divine law.

Apart from God there is no law. Apart from having an internal sense of right and wrong one will evolve to a lawless state. The state were moral law is ignored and in some cases completely abandoned is lawlessness. When you take the increase in lawlessness into consideration with what has happened in this nation, it explains why our society is declining.

Here is the stinger to this damming conclusion. There was a day and a time where leaders believed in a higher power, a moral law giver. So they at least had that as an internal check against themselves. As we have progressed there are leaders in the Church and in the government that sit in positions of authority who have no internal code that limits them or compels them to be moral. Where lawlessness comes in there is no compulsion to do what's right, instead there is a compulsion to do what feels good to them.

Former President Clinton in the early stages of his scandals did exhibit some sense of shame or remorse because of his belief in God. This did not stop him from doing what he did but he did exhibit some form of remorse. The principle degradation that comes with sin is that sin progresses to its end, death. In this case, death is complete separation from God.

There are those who have a hatred for authority in general. Even though the people who have a hatred for authority sit in offices of authority, this disrespect for authority is felt in the atmosphere around these people. This atmosphere is a breeding ground that fosters an attitude of disregard for authority. This seems contradictory but we see evidence of this with Former President Obama. Obama had a hatred for authority and that opened the door for many evil things to take place. If the chief person in authority has no regard for authority what happens to those under them?

At very basic levels it has been well documented that former President Obama showed great levels of contempt for authority, especially Christian authority. This disrespect for Christianity and even the authority of the Bible drove the policies of his administration. It is the fundamental groundwork for the antichrist spirit according to the Apostle John. In the days ahead, the antichrist spirit will have a major influence on the World, not just the United States. Obama laid the foundation for the antichrist to be able to operate in the United States. Antichrist and lawlessness are synonymous. This lawlessness started with an attack on the police.

> "It seemed to me that Obama had a unique opportunity to speak about values and virtues to this minority of African Americans—to tell them that his own life exemplified how in twenty-first century America you could get an education, work hard, get married, be an attentive husband

and father, and maybe even become president of the United States.

How disappointing that he chose the other tack, stoking grievance and resentment over supposed victimization by all authority, whether from teachers, cops, or potential employers. He and his attorneys general went sniffing out evidences of racism everywhere, and demonizing the police. Even after five officers were assassinated by an enraged black murderer in Dallas, he said, inaccurately, falsely, and callously: "There are legitimate issues that have been raised, and there's data and evidence to back up the concerns that are being expressed by these [Black Lives Matter] protesters."[vii]

Myron Magnet speaks to the hope that many people thought Obama was gonna bring to this Nation. Instead he pushed an agenda of racial inequality and used the police as the targets to spread racial disharmony. The people who voted for him had a desire to see an end to racial tension. The antichrist spirit does not want to end racial tension, the antichrist spirit wants to keep that racial tension alive.

Like every profession there are bad apples among the good. However, you cannot argue with what appears to be a systematic attack against the police. If the President of the United States does not demonstrate a respect for the police, every day citizens will not. The antichrist spirit caused a calculated, planned assault on authority.

In 2014, after a grand jury found no evidence to indict Officer Darren Wilson for the death of Michael Brown in Ferguson, Missouri, Obama shared publicly that he believes the police were discriminatory.

"The law too often feels like it's being applied in a discriminatory fashion... Communities of color aren't just making these problems up... These are real issues. And we have to lift them up and not deny them or try to tamp them down. *Speech by former President Obama November 2014*"viii

When all was said and done the system found Officer Darren Wilson innocent. Obama found fault with the system and attacked the system. The antichrist spirit in Obama is actively working to destroy authority. The media aided in causing incorrect information to come out into the public and further point the finger of blame at authority rather than deal with the situation for what it was. The point here is that because the person in authority did not have regard for other authority that disrespect transferred into other people.

In May 2015, in the Bronx, the president asserted: "The law is not always applied evenly in this country. [Young black men] experience being treated differently by law enforcement—in stops and in arrests, and in charges and incarcerations. The statistics are clear, up and down the criminal justice system. There's no dispute. *Speech by former President Obama May 2015*"ix

This attack against authority was very clear. Division took place through the hands of the antichrist spirit. Race relations were supposed to improve under President Obama instead they worsened. More people saw color than they saw the actual facts and circumstances surrounding the events that took place during the scandals with the police while President Obama was in office. The media and its cohorts magnified anything that was related to race. This made for some very big public relations nightmares for the police.

There were accusations of intentional brutality by the police and the Obama administration made sure to highlight these cases. The brutality was not factual but that was never reported by the media. Former President Obama went after

25 police departments over his administration. He went after the Sanford, Florida police department with the Trayvon Martin shooting. This had nothing to do with that police department because the shooter, George Zimmerman was was not an officer. In February 2016, Obama's Justice Department sued the City of Ferguson, Missouri. The Justice Department found the police department guilty of racism without ever checking the racial crime rates of the City of Ferguson. This is mandatory in order to establish probable cause but in his administration, the police were deemed guilty before a trial was ever held. This fueled the fires of hatred toward the police.

"Harvard professor and noted African American scholar Henry Louis Gates Jr. was arrested at his home in Cambridge, Mass., spawning an acrimonious national debate about racial profiling. A few days later, Obama, for the first time in his presidency, stumbled into a race debate from which his image as a racial healer has never recovered. His approval rating among white men plummeted, never to rebound.

"I don't know, not having been there and not seeing all the facts, what role race played in that," Obama said after Gates's arrest. "But I think it's fair to say, number one, any of us would be pretty angry; number two, that the Cambridge police acted stupidly in arresting somebody when there was already proof that they were in their own home, and, number three, what I think we know separate and apart from this incident is that there's a long history in this country of African Americans and Latinos being stopped by law enforcement disproportionately.""[x]

Attacks against the police have taken place in the name of "Social Justice". These attacks have been orchestrated behind the scenes by those who are working to create an atmosphere that is anti-authority. These attacks were headed up by the Office of the President constituted an attack on the moral fiber of this nation. You have to look at the source. Whoever heard of the Commander-in-chief taking up such an attack against authority? Many people in the secular world believed it was a conspiracy of some sorts but the Church did not raise this concern. The Church remained silent.

The next attack was on the military. This attack had to do with our authority and how we as a nation were being portrayed around the world. At the beginning of Obama's time in Office he immediately began taking trips around the world. These trips were in his eyes for the purpose of improving the image of the United States around the world. What did he do? He apologized to the world for our Nation being a superpower. Former President Obama said, "That our past foreign policy decisions had contributed negatively to the rest of the world not being able to get out of poverty and take care of their own people.

The apologies did not end there. Former President Obama apologized to the World because we detained the enemy combatants in Guantanamo Bay. Former President Obama apologized for how our Nation prosecuted the war on Terror. He apologized for how CIA interrogation techniques were conducted. He apologized to the Muslim world for this Nations colonialism. He apologized to France and Europe, saying that we allowed our Alliance to drift apart. He apologized at the Summit of Americas stating that we were disengaged because we had so much wealth. He apologized at the G-20 Summit in 2009, he accused this Nation of being dictators. His apology tour made us look weak as a Nation.

"Look at how long it took the President to recognize the threat from ISIS terrorists. And once he acknowledged the threat, Obama telegraphed our every move; announcing the air campaign, announcing the air attacks in Syria and saying that the first attacks there were going to be the hardest. He has also repeated, like a mantra, that there would be no American 'boots on the ground' although most military leaders say that ISIS cannot be defeated by air power alone and that Iraqi and Kurdish infantry and Syrian rebels might not be able to defeat ISIS on the ground.[xi]

Many veterans and veterans groups tried to give Obama the benefit of the doubt but it became very clear what he thought about our military. He did some pretty brazen things that signaled disrespect on all levels. So many supporters of Obama made excuses for his behavior and some claimed that it was just his laid back attitude. The truth is that his actions were deliberate and went against what standard protocol is for any President. (See photos).

In these photo's (Larry Patriot)[xii] Obama did not follow typical American protocol. He stood in a position that disrespected military tradition. He did not place his hand over his heart and he had the appearance of not participating in this part of the ceremony.

You can make excuses for someone when they do not know but there is an officer (Chief of Protocol) that works for the United States Department of State who is responsible for advising all presidents on national and international diplomatic protocol.

In the beginning he could claim that he did not know but his Chief of Protocol gave him the information he needed. He chose to disregard that information. This assault on the police and military people coupled with the bad character of our presidents is directly responsible for the changes in viewpoint that our people have towards authority. This is a strategic attack by the antichrist spirit.

Veterans were constantly being smeared and even listed as potential terrorists. He blamed our troops for the Taliban attacking the United States because our troops supported women's rights, walked in front of Muslims while they were praying, and our troops did not wear latex gloves when handling the Koran. He publicly stated the Fort Hood

Massacre of thirteen soldiers, one who was pregnant was an act of workplace violence not terrorism because the assailant was a Muslim.

Major-General Harold J. Greene, the highest-ranking officer to be killed on foreign soil, was not important enough for Obama to cancel a round of golf so that he could attend the funeral. Former President Obama wanted civilian and military personnel to wear clothing in observance of Ramadan while they were in Bahrain, Persian Gulf in 2014. In 2013 Former President Obama made it a court-martial offense if anyone of the Christian faith was caught proselytizing or inducing someone to convert to Christianity. Also In 2013 at a U.S. Army briefing he placed "Evangelical Christianity" and "Catholicism" on the same list as Al-Qaeda, Muslim Brotherhood, and Hamas as examples of "religious extremism."

The Secret Service was affected by this. Things became so bad that it directly affected the Secret Service. There was so much disrespect towards authority that for the first time in our history those who were tasked with the responsibility of guarding the president began to be involved in some very high-profile scandals. These scandals illustrate the effects of this attack on authority from within. This disrespect for authority created an atmosphere that created a lack of discipline and a sense of chaos amongst the ranks. Anyone could do anything and not to be held accountable.

There have been many reports of misconduct among the rank & file members of the Secret Service. As of 2015 there were at least 143[xiii] security breaches or attempted breaches at facilities secured by the Secret Service. A government reform committee was established, and they reported that the Secret Service was an "agency in crisis". There were a series of high-profile embarrassments that caused the eye of the public to be placed upon these officers.

"Morale is down, attrition is up, misconduct continues, and security breaches persist. Strong leadership from the top is required to fix the systemic mismanagement within the agency and to restore it to its former prestige."[xiv]

Here is a list of some of the indiscretions that took place:

1. *In 2011, agents allow gunman, Oscar Ortega-Hernandez to shoot at and penetrate the White House.*
2. *In 2012 agents were sent home from a presidential trip to Colombia for misconduct involving prostitutes.*
3. *In 2013 an agent left a bullet in the room of a Washington Hotel.*
4. *In 2014 three agents were sent home from a presidential trip to the Netherlands because they were found passed out drunk in Amsterdam, Netherlands.*
5. *In 2014 an armed security guard is allowed to get on an elevator with Obama. It was only after the man was taking pictures with his cell phone that they realized their mistake.*
6. *In 2014 Omar Gonzalez leaps over the White House fence, runs through the front door of the executive mansion (which was unlocked) and moves through most of the bottom floor. Then months later a second man jumps the fence again.*
7. *In 2014 the agent that investigated the agents involved in the prostitution in 2012 was forced to resign himself because of being involved in prostitution in Florida.*
8. *In 2015 two drunken agents run into a security barrier then proceeded through a secured area during an active bomb investigation.*

Clearly there is something wrong with these incidents listed above. It just shows the effects of what has occurred because of the disintegration of leadership from the Office of the President. There is a lot of responsibility by the person who holds that office.

What is at stake is there is an abomination that is going on. This abomination is leaving a void within the structure of this nation. People do not know what to think of it. People do not know what it is that is going on. They feel the darkness; they feel the chaos but all at the same time the enemy has been allowed to come through open doors in our leadership. Open doors that have invited other negative spirits and influences with it to bring an assault against Godly authority. This war that is being waged is being fought by the antichrist himself and his forces.

.

2 Types of Kings – Chapter 2
What God Has Said

> Do you see how they are making a sham out of their king that I have chosen... they are totally disrespecting the Capitol just as they totally disrespect My throne.
> **By Pastor/Evangelist Barbara Lynch (2019)**

The statement above is a prophetic word that the Holy Spirit through God shared with my pastor. I believe that it speaks to a fundamental issue that is a sign of how far our society has strayed from the norms of decency and civility.

When God speaks about "Their king that I have chosen" that is a reference to an actual Old Testament event that took place after the Nation of Israel rejected God from being their King. This event took place in 1st Samuel Chapter 8 of the Bible. There was a prophet of God named Samuel who was advancing in years. He was a Godly man, but his sons did not walk in his ways.

The Bible says that Samuel's sons Joel and Abijah were judges of the Nation of Israel and they were wicked. Joel and Abijah turned aside after dishonest gain, took bribes, and perverted justice. Unfortunately, this sounds like some of the Judges that we have today in the United States. The people of Israel saw how they were, and they went to Samuel and told him that they had a better way and that better way was for God to give them a king.

The people of this Nation wanted to have a king over them. As they went to Samuel and made their demand for a king. God saw what was going on and told Samuel to appoint a king over them but God said to the people this king will not treat you right. Even after God warned them and told them this king will be bad for you. They did not care, they wanted what they wanted. So God gave them exactly what they wanted.

There are times when God will give you what you ask for even though it is not good for you. This is the case here with the nation of Israel. The reality of what the Nation of Israel asked for boiled down to them in effect rejecting God. They were telling God that they did not want Him as their king. The pattern that God was trying to set up for them was a pattern of having a direct relationship with Him. They missed God.

In this case they got a man, King Saul. Saul was the people's choice. Saul was self-centered, self-focused, arrogant, proud, and he did not have a heart that beat after God. King Saul's ways brought the Nation of Israel into bondage and captivity. This captivity caused loss of life and loss of closeness with God. Saul was a bad king.

In contrast with the Nation of Israel in more recent years the United States had a prophetic King Saul over it. The people had a choice to pick a candidate who was more like God and less like the devil. Mitt Romney was supposed to be Republican presidential nominee in 2008 but he was beat out by John McCain. Evangelicals did not vote in the primary because the Church opted out because they did not want to vote for a Mormon. I believe if the Church would have been listening to God, Romney would have been 2008 President. When the Church does not act from God's perspective a mess is created. God wanted Romney but the people chose Obama.

The wrong choice was made, and Barack Obama entered office in 2008. Barack Obama did more to destroy the heritage and the foundations of this nation than any president in our history. Looking back, I believe that many Christians realized that they should have voted for Romney. As we look back now, we can clearly see that Obama came in the door with an agenda from the devil. That agenda was to dismantle the godly foundation of this nation. Obama came in the door apologizing for our heritage and trying to rewrite the history of this nation by ascribing that this nation was built on the principles of Islam. This Nation was not founded on the principles of Islam.

"Which passages of scripture should guide our public policy? Should we go with, Leviticus which suggests slavery is okay? Or we can go with, we could go with Deuteronomy, which suggests stoning your child if he strays from the faith? Or should we just stick to the Sermon on the Mount? A passage that is so radical that it's doubtful that our own Defense Department would survive its application. Folks haven't been reading the Bible." *Speech by former Senator Obama June 28th, 2006*[xv]

"Moreover, given the increasing diversity of America's population, the dangers of sectarianism have never been greater. Whatever we once were, we are no longer just a Christian nation; we are also a Jewish nation, a Muslim nation, a Buddhist nation, a Hindu nation, and a nation of nonbelievers. And even if we did have only Christians in our midst, if we expelled every non-Christian from the United States of America, whose Christianity would we teach in the schools? Would we go with James Dobson's, or Al Sharpton's? *Speech by former Senator Obama June 28, 2006[xvi]*

"I've said before that one of the great strengths of the United States is although as I mentioned we have a very large Christian population <u>we do not consider ourselves a Christian nation</u> or a Jewish nation or a Muslim nation we consider ourselves a nation of citizens who are bound by ideals and a set of values" *Speech by former President Obama to Turkey April 6, 2009.[xvii]*

Everyone mocked and ridiculed the leaders of the Church who raised a flag against Obamas straight forward and direct claims that the United States was no longer a "Christian" nation. Nothing was by chance when it came to how Obama spoke or delivered a message. Obama chose his words very carefully. Many were deceived by this rhetoric. He meant what he said and for the first time since the founding of this nation an American president, an insider, snubbed our Judeo-Christian heritage. It was done in such a way that only those who were observant caught on.

His dismissiveness of our Judeo-Christian heritage coupled with his love of Islam would relegate this nations Christians to eight years of political repression and oppression. His desire to promote secularism and freedom from religion, opened the door for what began as an open assault on Christianity in this nation. What became extremely clear to those in the Christian and Jewish communities was that Obama was serious about convincing people that what he believed was the truth. The effects of his persuasiveness are still being felt today. He became a god to many who followed his ideology.

Obama started multiplying the lie that this nation was not a Christian nation. While it had a powerful effect upon citizens of this nation, the Islamic world did not accept his ideology. The Islamic world still saw this Nation as a threat to its future ability to exist. There is not now, nor will there ever be a plan for co-existence.

"According to a recent Pew poll, only 22 percent of Egyptians believe the United States played a positive role in their uprising. In the same poll, more Egyptians, remarkably, said they approved of both al Qaeda and Osama bin Laden than they did the United States.   Obviously, these sentiments are not solely tied to America's support for Mubarak, but it is a major factor contributing to still considerable mistrust toward the United States."[xviii]

This took place after the Arab Spring uprising took place in the Middle East in 2012 approximately four years after Obama became President.

"As for those who actually live in the Middle East, a less militaristic America has done little to temper anti-Americanism.   In the three countries—Egypt, Jordan, and Lebanon—for which Pew has survey data for both Bush's last year and either 2014 or 2015, favorability toward the U.S. is significantly worse under Obama today than it was in 2008. Why exactly is up for debate, but we can at the very least say that a drastic drawdown of U.S. military personnel—precisely the policy pushed for by Democrats in the wake of Iraq's failure—does not seem to have bought America much goodwill."[xix]

This article was written in October of 2016 at the end of Obamas term.   It reveals an interesting truth about the Islamic world. Those who practice radical Islam do not like this Nation. Obama gutted this nation's military, ran our foreign policy with the intent of showing the world we were sorry for our political sins, and the Islamists were still not satisfied. The radical Islamists will only be happy with this Nations non-existence.

Obama's error in believing that he could change the world's view of our Nation by denying its heritage drew out more error in the Church. Many people thought that Obama was the actual antichrist spirit incarnated. This is/was not true nor is it biblical. Obama is/was not the antichrist. This split the Church on so many levels.

> Obama is not the antichrist but he is
> paving the way for the antichrist spirit to come.
> **By Evangelist/Pastor Barbara Lynch (2007)**

The above statement was a prophetic word that the Holy Spirit through God spoke to Pastor Barbara. The Body of Christ because of its failure to know Bible prophecy completely missed what was happening in the Spirit realm. They were blind to God's truth so they were unable to see long term and long range at what the enemy's strategy is for this nation.

Obama opened the door for the antichrist spirit to be embedded in the highest levels of government in our time. He did this because he himself believes that Jesus is just a historical figure. Obama was asked by a reporter who Jesus was to him, this is what his response was.

> "He immediately responded with a nervous laugh, followed by a rather sarcastic "Right." He proceeded, "Jesus is an historical figure for me, and he's also a bridge between God and man, in the Christian faith, and one that I think is powerful precisely because he serves as that means of us reaching something higher. And he's also a wonderful teacher."[xx]

Jesus is not just a wonderful teacher. He is the anointed Son of the most-high God. Obama denied that Jesus is the anointed Son of the most-high God. You can sugar coat this all you want but the Bible is clear.

> ²By this you know and recognize the Spirit of God: every spirit that acknowledges and confesses [the fact] that Jesus Christ has [actually] come in the flesh [as a man] is from God [God is its source]; ³and every spirit that does not confess Jesus [acknowledging that He has come in the flesh, but would deny any of the Son's true nature] is not of God; this is the spirit of the antichrist, which you have heard is coming, and is now already in the world.
>
> **1 John 4: 2 - 3 (AMP)**

There were many documented incidents where Obama acted cold and indifferent to Christians and Jews who sought an audience with him to help resolve issues or terror or violence against Christians or Jews. In each case Obama sided with whatever group that was favorable to Islam. If he were really a Christian as he pretended to be. Why the cold shoulder to them? Why treat them with contempt?

> "According to research showing the links between Presidential adviser Dalia Mogahed and the Muslim Brotherhood, and to NGOs representing Middle East Christian groups in the US, blocking Middle East Christian meetings at the White House and the State Department have been associated with the work of the "advisors" and their allies in the Islamist camp in Washington such as CAIR and MPAC.
>
> Coptic Solidarity International which has been trying to obtain meetings at the White House or with Secretary Clinton at State to expose the horrors committed against the Christian Copts of Egypt, were not granted such access. Also and despite the many massacres against Christians in

Iraq over the past two years, representatives from the Assyro-Chaldeans of the US were not received in the Oval Office or by Secretary Clinton, at a time Islamist linked groups are on the roster of invitations to the White House. Indicatively, Administration officials declined invitations to speak at the annual Assyrian Christian convention this year, few months from the start of the withdrawal from Iraq.[xxi]

Obama was not the antichrist but there was strong evidence by his policies and behaviors that he was not sympathetic to Christians or Jews. Obama and his policies the antichrist spirit gained ground in this nation because people in the Church did not want to call evil, Evil. Christians were afraid of being called racist and this kept many from speaking the truth.

It is not an act of a Christian to do the things that Obama did to the Christians and Jews that Obama encountered. The Church has to stop tip-toeing around this truth. Obama showed no mercy towards Christians or Jews. This is who Obama is. Obama used his influence and power to change policies in favor of Muslims and against Christians.

April 2008 – Obama speaks disrespectfully of Christians, saying they "cling to guns or religion" and have an "antipathy to people who aren't like them."

May 2009 – While Obama does not host any National Day of Prayer event at the White House, he does host White House Iftar dinners in honor of Ramadan.

2010 – While every White House traditionally issues hundreds of official proclamations and statements on numerous occasions, this White House avoids traditional Biblical holidays and events but regularly recognizes major Muslim holidays, as evidenced by its 2010 statements on Ramadan, Eid-ul-Fitr, Hajj, and Eid-ul-Adha.

October 2011 – The Obama administration eliminates federal grants to the U.S. Conference of Catholic Bishops for their extensive programs that aid victims of human trafficking because the Catholic Church is anti-abortion.

December 2012 – Despite having campaigned to recognize Jerusalem as Israel's capital, President Obama once again suspends the provisions of the Jerusalem Embassy Act of 1995 which requires the United States to recognize Jerusalem as the capital of Israel and to move the American Embassy there.

April 2013 – The United States Agency for Internal Development (USAID), an official foreign policy agency of the U.S. government, begins a program to train homosexual activists in various countries around the world to overturn traditional marriage and anti-sodomy laws, targeting first those countries with strong Catholic influences, including Ecuador, Honduras, and Guatemala.

June 2014 – Official U. S. government personnel, both civilian and military, in Bahrain (a small Arabic nation near Saudi Arabia, Iraq, and Iran) must wear clothing that facilitates the religious observance of the Islamic holy month of Ramadan.

March 2015 – A decorated Navy chaplain was prohibited from fulfilling his duty of comforting the family (or any member of the unit) after the loss of a sailor because it was feared that he would say something about faith and God. He was even banned from the base on the day of the sailor's memorial service.

April 2016 – At the orders of a commander, a 33-year Air Force veteran was forcibly and physically removed by four other airmen because he attempted to use the word "God" in a retirement speech. [xxii]

Obama went to a church that practices anti-Semitism. He was not a friend of Israel and he did not miss any opportunity to show the world his attitude against Israel. Obama started the trends towards disrespecting authority. He did not show respect for the police or the military in fact he gutted the military over his time in office.

During his presidency he launched ruthless attacks on our veterans by cancelling or reducing the health care benefits of those who served, reducing their benefits, and making a public mockery of them. He placed rules and restrictions upon them so that they were unable to properly prosecute any of the wars against Islamic nations or powers. Many lives were lost because of these rules and regulations. He forbid any negative press against Muslims.

Obama opened the door for the Muslim Brotherhood to enter the highest levels of our government. They came in with a plan to destroy us from the inside out. Many of them are still hidden inside strategic parts of our government and today they are causing President Trump grief and havoc. Obama was blatantly open about his hatred and disdain for this nation at home and when he went abroad. He was so open about what he was doing that many were surprised when he won a second term as President.

Obama did not hide anything that he believed. This should have been a sign to the Church that something was off and had shifted but the Church was going through its own internal crisis. Nonetheless this was a sign that the hearts of the American people were in the midst of a change towards darkness. It would be different if the American people were tricked by Obama but they weren't. They wanted him in office. Which proves that they wanted this king and what he provided to them.

To this day, many are swayed by the persuasive deceptiveness of the spirit behind this man. Those who are dark spiritually want Obamas way of life. They still swoon after him. Even now many people are talking about giving him a third term. This is not constitutional, but many people are talking about convincing his wife to run for the Presidency. (...at the time of this writing she has refused but who knows what will happen.)

So how this ties together with the prophetic word is that the season for Obamas' presidency completed an eight-year term of being under the king that this nation chose. There was intercession that took place during that eight-year period and God granted us grace. This grace allowed for President Trump to be elected. This opened the door for God to place the king over us that He chose. God wants us to be led by President Donald Trump.

This really is God's grace but it is also proving how much the people in this nation do not want God. The saddest part about this is how people are rejecting God. Just like the Nation of Israel, they are rejecting President Trump. They do not understand that by coming against President Trump they are coming against God.

The level of disrespect that people are showing towards President Trump continues to escalate. The disrespect is not warranted; however, as believers we must keep at the forefront of our minds that the enemy has a stronghold in place for those who have accepted Jesus Christ as Lord and Savior. We are losing the battle in this area because the Church has taken on the mindset of the world.

We must see the battle for what it really is. President Trump is subject to unnecessary warfare from the principalities and powers who are working against God's plan to revitalize this nation. There have been many strange notions that Christians believe have to be true about the President of the United States. They are not founded in scripture.

One of the strangest notions is that our presidents has to be a Bible thumping, Spirit filled, tongue talking, Gospel gangster type in order for God's purposes to be completed. This is not true, nor is it biblical. Many leaders in the Church are upset with President Trump because he does not fit into this Christian personality type.

President Trump will never fit into this personality type and the church must grow up in their understanding of God and how He works. History has proven that God can use any vessel. That vessel does not need to be anointed, religious, speaking in tongues, or prophesying in order for God's purposes to be accomplished.

> [3] "Listen! Behold, a sower went out to sow. [4] And it happened, as he sowed, *that* some *seed* fell by the wayside; and the birds of the air came and devoured it. [5] Some fell on stony ground, where it did not have much earth; and immediately it sprang up because it had no depth of earth.
>
> [6] But when the sun was up it was scorched, and because it had no root it withered away. [7] And some *seed* fell among thorns; and the thorns grew up and choked it, and it yielded no crop. [8] But other *seed* fell on good ground and yielded a crop that sprang up, increased and produced: some thirtyfold, some sixty, and some a hundred."
>
> **Mark 4: 3 – 8 (NKJV)**

God talks about 30, 60, and a 100 fold people in scripture. In all of these cases God proves that His hand is upon these people. He never rejects anyone who has a heart that's open to God. This is where the Church has improperly judged President Trump. They do not know his heart and they are trying to make him fit in a mold that God does not want him in. Thus the limitation that has been placed upon President Donald Trump is not valid.

We are expecting for our viewpoint of how we think he should live to place limitations upon what God can do. It is a form of jealousy. Christians are mad at him because he does not behave according to the standard that they have set up for themselves. What should be occurring is President Trump receiving more grace to do his job but what winds up happening is an unfair amount of criticism and ridicule that is not coming from the anointing. There is a purpose, there is a plan that God is in control of and the world does not like President Donald Trump because he is God's man.

> ¹Now Elisha the prophet called one of the sons of the prophets and said to him, "Gird up your loins (prepare for action), take this flask of oil in your hand and go to Ramoth-gilead. ² When you arrive there, look for Jehu the son of Jehoshaphat the son of Nimshi, and go in and have him arise from among his brothers, and take him into an inner room. ³ Then take the flask of oil and pour it on his head and say, 'Thus says the Lord: "I have anointed you king over Israel."' Then open the door and flee and do not delay."
>
> ⁶ So Jehu got up, and they went into the house. And he poured the oil on Jehu's head and said to him, "Thus says the Lord, the God of Israel: 'I have anointed you king over the people of the Lord, over Israel. ⁷ You shall strike the house of Ahab your master, so that I may avenge the blood of My servants the prophets, and the blood of all the servants of the Lord, [who have died] at the hands of

Jezebel. **8** For the entire house of Ahab shall perish, and I will cut off from Ahab every male, both bond and free, in Israel.

2 Kings 9: 1 – 3, 6 – 8 (AMP)

Whether you want to accept this or not President Trump is operating under the anointing that God has given him. God has given President Trump a Jehu anointing. This is an anointing that specializes in taking down the ahab and jezebel spirit. The ahab and jezebel spirit is the spirit that has allowed the antichrist spirit to set up a strong hold in this nation. Because jezebel practiced idolatry and ahab was tolerant of idol worship, Ahab allowed for all kinds of false religions to come into this nation. Things are deeper in the Spirit realm than you can ever imagine.

If the Body of Christ is going to be effective for God we must stop placing limitations upon Him. God can and will continue to use whomever He wants to use for His purposes. In spite of the Church God is moving forward with His agenda. As a body of believers, we are committing the same errors and misunderstandings of God that the Jewish people made.

The Jewish people did not understand God either. They believed that God was sending Jesus as a King the first time. They did not understand the plan or intentions of God and the Church is of like mind and just as dull in heart. The Church is missing what God is really doing through the hands and the heart of President Donald Trump.

Many in the Jewish community believe President Trump to be of the same nature and character as the Persian King Cyrus of the Old Testament. As Netanyahu explained in his remarks on March 5, 2018 at a Press Conference in the White House:

I want to tell you that the Jewish people have a long memory, so we remember the proclamation of the great king, Cyrus the Great, the Persian king 2,500 years ago. He proclaimed that the Jewish exiles in Babylon could come back and rebuild our Temple in Jerusalem. We remember a hundred years ago, Lord Balfour, who issued the Balfour Proclamation that recognized the rights of the Jewish people in our ancestral homeland. We remember 70 years ago, President Harry S. Truman was the first leader to recognize the Jewish state. And we remember how a few weeks ago, President Donald J. Trump recognized Jerusalem as Israel's capital. Mr. President, this will be remembered by our people through the ages. *Speech by Benjamin Netanyahu 2019*[xxiii]

Photo of Prime Minister Netanyahu with President Trump - January 2018[xxiv]

Immediately after President Trump entered office, he began working to restore the relationship between Israel and The United States. He put forth plans to move our embassy from Tel Aviv to Jerusalem. He put action to his words by not only pledging support for Israel but being vocal about compelling other nations to stand with Israel.

In December of 2017, the United Nations voted on and signed a resolution to declare Jerusalem "null and void" as the capital of Israel. As a result, 128 countries voted for the measure while only 9 voted against. The United States, a handful of Pacific island nations, and a few Central American countries voted against it. He has been vocal about Israel's right to exist as a Nation. He fits the pattern that Prime Minister Netanyahu spoke about.

Let's look at some of the things Cyrus did as King over Persia. As we do this let's draw out some comparisons and contrasts of the lives of the Children of Israel. I believe it is here that you will see in types and shadows what God is really doing and how God is really moving. It is here that you will understand it is God's protocol to bring honor back to the Nation of Israel. He is bringing honor back to the Office of the Presidency of the United States.

Cyrus was responsible for beginning the great Persian Empire. His empire lasted for two hundred years. It was destroyed by Alexander the Great. We know from history that Cyrus was born between 590 and 580 BCE, most likely in the area known as the Fars province in Iran. There are many legends that surround Cyrus' family one of the more popular legends is the one that Cyrus was given while a shepherd to raise in a similar way that Moses was placed in the bulrushes in Egypt.

The true meaning of Cyrus name is one of historical dispute. The question surrounds his name as being where the original personal name or the name given to him as he ascended his throne. When Cyrus became the ruler of Persia. The name does not appear anymore throughout the empire so there is a specialty ascribe to Cyrus. To put it briefly Cyrus was the Great Grandfather of the great king Cyrus. He came from a long line of ruling chiefs. His family testimony is that they were capable of founding the Persian Empire with strength that would last for two centuries.

God has already purposed President Donald Trump to help bring things together with the Nation of Israel. This is God's appointed time to raise Israel up in stature. President Trump was used by God to not only declare that Jerusalem is the capital of Israel, but he moved the United States Embassy from Tel Aviv to Jerusalem.

He put action to his words. This one act alone proves beyond a shadow of a doubt that God is using President Trump to fulfill His purposes in the Earth. There are many things that are going on behind the scenes that I do not believe God will reveal until He is ready, and they may not be until we have reached the other side of eternity. The Scriptures are plain.

> [22] Now in the first year of Cyrus king of Persia, that the word of the Lord by the mouth of Jeremiah might be fulfilled, the Lord stirred up the spirit of Cyrus king of Persia, so that he made a proclamation throughout all his kingdom, and also *put it* in writing, saying,
>
> [23] Thus says Cyrus king of Persia: All the kingdoms of the earth the Lord God of heaven has given me. And He has commanded me to build Him a house at Jerusalem which is in Judah. Who *is* among you of all His people? May the Lord his God *be* with him, and let him go up!
>
> **2 Chronicles 36: 22 – 23 (NKJV)**

> Who says of Cyrus, '*He is* My shepherd, and he shall perform all My pleasure, saying to Jerusalem, "You shall be built," and to the temple, "Your foundation shall be laid."'
>
> **Isaiah 44: 28 (NKJV)**

> [1]"Thus says the Lord to His anointed, to Cyrus, whose right hand I have held— to subdue nations before him and loose the armor of kings, to open before him the double doors, so that the gates will not be shut: [2] 'I will go before you and make the crooked places straight; I will break in pieces the gates of bronze and cut the bars of iron.
>
> [3] I will give you the treasures of darkness and hidden riches of secret places, that you may know that I, the

Lord, who call *you* by your name, *Am* the God of Israel. [4] For Jacob My servant's sake, and Israel My elect, I have even called you by your name; I have named you, though you have not known Me.

Isaiah 45: 1 – 4 (NKJV)

Cyrus was chosen by God to bring Israel out of captivity. God spoke this in Isaiah 44: 28. Isaiah predicted that Cyrus would free the Nation of Israel one hundred fifty years before Cyrus lived. God's word does not lie. It is accurate to a fault.

God moved upon Cyrus heart not only to return the Jews back to Israel, but he gave them back the items that were taken from them prior to them going into captivity. He restored the wealth and the riches of the priesthood. God set it up so they could continue to worship Him. God moved upon Cyrus heart to provide for the Nation of Israel. He permitted the building of the Temple with monies from Cyrus' treasury. Some historians credit Cyrus with starting Judaism.

[7] King Cyrus also brought out the articles of the house of the Lord, which Nebuchadnezzar had taken from Jerusalem and put in the temple of his gods; [8] and Cyrus king of Persia brought them out by the hand of Mithredath the treasurer, and counted them out to Sheshbazzar the prince of Judah.

Ezra 1: 7 – 8 (NKJV)

[4] *with* three rows of heavy stones and one row of new timber. Let the expenses be paid from the king's treasury. [5] Also let the gold and silver articles of the house of God, which Nebuchadnezzar took from the temple which *is* in Jerusalem and brought to Babylon, be restored and taken back to the temple which *is* in Jerusalem, *each* to its place; and deposit *them* in the house of God"—

Ezra 6: 4 – 5 (NKJV)

Besides his dealings with the Jews, Cyrus is known for his advancement of human rights, his brilliant military strategy, and his bridging of Eastern and Western cultures. He was a king of tremendous influence and a person God used to help fulfill an important Old Testament prophecy. God's use of Cyrus as a "shepherd" for His people illustrates the truth of <u>Proverbs 21: 1</u>, "The king's heart is in the hand of the LORD; he directs it like a watercourse wherever he pleases."**xxv**

What many did not know prior to the 2016 election was that God handpicked President Trump to push Israel forward as a nation. Some mock and ridicule President Trump and consider him a heathen. This is similar in nature to what history records about Cyrus. Cyrus was a heathen but that did not stop him from being used by God to accomplish a mighty works for Him. This mockery of the authority that God has placed over us does not hinder or stop President Trump in the slightest. It will not stop God. Our nation is in trouble and the Church has to recognize that God has provided the king that we need to have to get us out of the messes that we are in. We cannot ignore what God is trying to do through President Trump.

Protocol – Chapter 3
Simple Things

Some leaders are born with the heart of a servant and others grow to become a servant through trials and tests. Like all politicians the President of the United States is called to be a servant to the people. The President has the responsibility of taking care of all of the citizens of this nation. Many have taken on this responsibility and become overwhelmed with the weight of power that is entrusted to them. That power crushes them and changes them. There are many influences that come against leaders in high offices, especially the President. Evil forces seek to use those whom they can in leadership and if they cannot use them then they do everything in their power to destroy them. This is what has been happening to President Trump. We, the Church, must intercede for him.

To date only 45 people have risen to be President of this nation. While many are envious of the power and authority that the position holds, many more understand that it is a job that it is filled with responsibility and weight that you cannot possibly imagine. There is a protocol to this office. This protocol is there to preserve the honor and dignity of the office. Over the years this protocol has been watered down by those who have held the position of President.

The case has been made that significant changes have taken place within this nation. These new "normals" have caused a shift in the protocols of how we the people as a nation operate. These changes in protocol have been occurring gradually behind the scenes for an extended period of time. They have reached the deepest core of the heart of this nation, the President. The tactics that the enemy uses are subtle and as the truth about the abomination that brings desolation is narrowed by the choices between two kings. God selected President Trump as a way to right the wrongs of past Presidents and give America another chance at greatness.

When you look at the history of this position, it is clear that the mindsets of past presidents has gone through a metamorphosis. From George Washington to Obama, great change has taken place. Those who have been seated in that office have migrated from a position of serving the people to serving themselves. Through a long process of corruption and demonic influence those who have stood as President over the United States have shifted to this perspective.

God has given us a fresh opportunity with President Trump to change this perspective and pattern. President Trump has given us an opportunity to change the course of this nation. President Trump has a heart to serve the people and do what is right. However, sin has brought corruption and the people's hearts have become darkened with perversity and every evil that is under the sun. This is a poison that has been injected into the spiritual realm over this nation. This poison can only be eradicated by the cleansing, saving grace of Jesus Christ. This grace has been secured by God, the Father, through President Trump.

Many political analysts do not see the spiritual aspects that are involved with serving this country. The ugly truth is the hearts of our politicians have changed from light to darkness. Our political leaders are a reflection of us. Our political leaders reflect the dark, cold nature of our hearts. We as a nation of people have become corrupted by darkness. We must cry out to God for Him to change our hearts.

God has performed many miracles for this country and down through the years our Presidents shared in the general populations reverence and honor of God. George Washington was a Godly, God fearing man. He was a devoted member of the Anglican Church, serving as the Church Warden for three terms.

> "...one former pastor at Pohick did state that "I never knew so constant an attendant at church as Washington." In general, Washington's religious life was filled with many seemingly contradictory positions.
>
> In regard to personal spirituality, Washington was generally private about his religious life. Washington is reported to have had regular private prayer sessions, and personal prayer was a large part of his life. One well-known report stated that Washington's nephew witnessed him doing personal devotions with an open Bible while kneeling, in both the morning and evening. It is clear that when it came to religion, Washington was a private man, more so than with other aspects of his life."[xxvi]

The protocol for George Washington was to be an upright person before God. This was not a requirement because he was President. This was a part of his inner nature and character. It was a part of who he was and that is what made him the great leader that Washington was in his day. God never intended for this nation to be a theocracy, but God did intend for the political leadership to live with honor and dignity before Him. Washington was better equipped to lead this nation because he had an inner moral guide.

There is an unbiblical teaching that has gone unchallenged for the past twenty years or more. It is the false doctrine of "Kingdom Now". The "Kingdom Now" doctrine teaches that all facets of the government will be taken over by the Church. They teach that Christians should seek political office to help facilitate Christ's return. There is an error in their understanding of scripture. The error fails to see that when Jesus returns the 2nd time, He is coming to destroy the corruption and sin that has prevailed over the earth. He is coming to destroy all ungodliness in the government and everywhere else. Many believe this false teaching because it puts the Church in charge of the world. This makes the Church a theocracy. To further add to the deception that is "Kingdom Now" they make this kingdom that is being set up American. It is not, it will be a world kingdom. Scripture is clear in Daniel 4, the kingdom that is well established on earth when Jesus returns is not the Church of God, it's the antichrist beast Kingdom that has taken over the whole world.

> 15 "I, Daniel, was grieved in my spirit within *my* body, and the visions of my head troubled me. 16 I came near to one of those who stood by, and asked him the truth of all this. So he told me and made known to me the interpretation of these things: 17 'Those great beasts, which are four, *are* four kings *which* arise out of the earth. 18 But the saints of the Most High shall receive the kingdom, and possess the kingdom forever, even forever and ever.'
> 19 "Then I wished to know the truth about the fourth beast, which was different from all the others, exceedingly dreadful, *with* its teeth of iron and its nails of bronze, *which* devoured, broke in pieces, and trampled the residue with

its feet; **20** and the ten horns that *were* on its head, and the other *horn* which came up, before which three fell, namely, that horn which had eyes and a mouth which spoke pompous words, whose appearance *was* greater than his fellows.

21 "I was watching; and the same horn was making war against the saints, and prevailing against them,

Daniel 7: 15 - 21 (NKJV)

So what "Kingdom Now" teaches is not scriptural. You see in verse 21 that Daniel saw these beings who were in control of the government when Christ returns. The government that is here when Christ returns will not be Godly. "Kingdom Now" asserts that we will hand the governments of this world over to Christ when He returns. Daniel also says that the government will be persecuting Christians.

Further down the line of the Presidency we find Abraham Lincoln. Lincoln had Godly character as well. Like others it is documented that he called the United States to three different times of fasting and prayer. Lincoln called for the nation to fast and pray to God so that we could have national peace and unity during the Civil War in 1861.

> "And I do earnestly recommend to all people, and especially to all ministers and teachers of religion, of all denominations, and to all heads of families, to observe and keep that day according to their several creeds and modes of worship, in all humility, and with all religious solemnity, to the end that the united prayer of the nation may ascend to the Throne of Grace, and bring down plentiful blessings upon our country. *Speech by former President Abraham Lincoln, 1861*"[xxvii]

Lincoln commissioned the people of this nation to seek God with prayer and fasting a second time in 1863. He believed that we as a nation needed to repent before God with prayer and fasting. How unprecedented is this for the President to call for such a humbling of hearts? Again, the honor of the person who was seated as president to act in such a way that would help the most people be free from the bondage that sin causes. Lincoln a third time called for fasting and prayer in 1864. This time he called for those in positions of authority to pray for clemency and forgiveness.

> "I do hereby further invite and request the heads of the executive departments of this government, together with all legislators, all judges and magistrates, and all other persons exercising authority in the land...and all the other law abiding people of the United States, to assemble in their preferred places of worship on that day, and there and then to render to the Almighty and merciful ruler of the universe such homages and such confessions. *Speech by former President Abraham Lincoln, 1863"*[xxviii]

As we fast forward to today. We can see that many things have changed in regards to politicians and what used to be called traditional moral values. Not all of them, but a good majority of the leaders are not living what we would consider Godly lifestyles at all. In fact, the lifestyles that they are living are the same as the constituents whom they represent. The line of demarcation has been crossed such that we have open sin being paraded in the White House.

We have laws on the books that forbid acts of perversion and lewdness but those laws are being changed. The ones aren't being changed are not being enforced. Remember the sex scandals that occurred with President Bill Clinton. George W. Bush was not an open adulterer but Bush did things to touch God's anointed, Israel. Because of what he did the United States went through some severe storms, Hurricane's Katrina and Rita. These storms caused severe destruction across our land. There were voices in the Church who spoke against the dividing up of Israel by Bush but that did not stop him from submitting to the will of the antichrist spirit.

And then came Obama which soon gave birth to a new spiritual climate of darkness over this land. The spiritual climate changed when the people elected Obama. We went into a time of spiritual famine and darkness. In Obama we had a king who knew not Joseph.

> [8]Now a new king arose over Egypt, who did not know Joseph [nor the history of his accomplishments]. [9]He said to his people, "Behold, the people of the sons of Israel are too many and too mighty for us [they greatly outnumber us]. [10]Come, let us deal shrewdly with them, so that they will not multiply and in the event of war, join our enemies, and fight against us and escape from the land."
> **Exodus 1: 8 – 10 (AMP)**

Obama did not want to know Joseph. Obama's background, his upbringing caused him to be fully immersed in the Islamic religion which is a manifestation of the antichrist spirit. Obama had been taught early on to not respect Joseph. Joseph was the son of Jacob referenced in Genesis chapters thirty seven to fifty who was sold into slavery by his brothers. Joseph was ordained by God to protect Israel and provide a way of escape for her during the world's deadliest famine. Joseph loved God and had a relationship with Him.

Because of Joseph the Nation of Israel was preserved. Through some unkind acts perpetrated against Joseph he was sold into slavery by his brothers and wound up in Egypt. Because Joseph was so favored of God, God used Joseph to save Israel and Egypt during this time of famine. During Obama's administration many evils were committed against Israel. It was no secret how Obama felt about them. This broke a long standing protocol that America would keep a strong relationship with Israel.

In contrast President Trump restored this relationship. President Trump repaired the breach that Obama placed between and Israel. President Trump may not do everything the way that people want him too but that does not take the anointing off of his life. Many people have misjudged and falsely accused him. They do not know his heart or that He is being used by God to complete certain prophetic promises that God has made to Israel. In contrast many hate President Trump but they love Obama. They love him because they are in agreement spiritually with the darkness that he walks in. Sad to say that many Church leaders and many prophetic people are just as dark. They did not understand the scriptures or the truth that Obama did not know Joseph.

The citizens who voted for Obama are not innocent but rather willing participants with Obama's sin. The citizens who voted for Obama failed to comprehend the darkness within Obama. They failed to separate themselves from that darkness and because of this they are literally fighting against God. These same people today are demonstrating that they do not want God in this nation. They are manifesting this attitude in the political realm and our nation is paying the price for this spiritually. The love affair with President Obama and his policies shows where the heart of the people who voted for him is. Many in the Church are just as in love with Obama today as they were when he was in Office. Despite what many propheliers said, Obama's heart was as cold as Pharaohs and the coldness in Obama's heart is a reflection of the darkness of the people of this nation.

9-11 was a wakeup call from God to the people of this nation. God allowed His protective hedge to drop around this nation. We were attacked by the antichrist spirit and thousands of people died physically, while untold thousands died spiritually. Even in this attack God's grace prevented more tragedy. After everything had unfolded it was revealed that the antichrist spirit had a plan for a total of twenty planes to be high jacked. God's grace permitted four to cause destruction that devastated America. We must come to grips with the truth that far more people would have died but God gave us mercy.

What is interesting was the response from the Church. After 9-11, Churches everywhere were packed out. Worldly people everywhere knew this was a sign of the times, but the Church came out with their false doctrine that _"God would never judge us because we are the great United States"_ and the move towards repentance to God was stopped. There was a mini outbreak of revival but the Church killed it by not telling the truth about the antichrist spirit.

Evangelist Rodney Howard-Browne, from South Africa, was holding crusades in New York prior to 9-11 and God showed Browne that something terrible was going to happen in New York. Many people attended these crusades and were touched by God, but the Church did not support and get behind what God was going through him. Many Church leaders came against him, mocked him and ridiculed him because of the "laughing revival" God was using Browne to bring Revival to the United States. Sad to say the repentance that was starting to grow and change people ended. The Church shut down the voice of God by attacking His true prophets and the people of this nation who were moved to repent, quickly went back out into the world never to return to Church.

It was then that the cloud of darkness quickly spread over this nation. While we who were going through the Clinton and Bush presidencies storm clouds of darkness began forming. These storm clouds transformed into a hedge of darkness during the Obama years. As the Obama presidency revealed itself for what it was the darkness became a shroud over this nation. It is then that we who started to see the most dramatic attacks upon morality and Godliness. This transformed how this nation was operated.

The answer was obvious but the Church closed its mouth and would not let the truth come out. In the name of not being judgmental. The light in the Church receded and pure darkness prevailed. People went to the Church, the Church denied the power of God, and then satan came in with full strength darkness that overtook our land. The Church was given times and seasons to repent and turn around to God but they refused.

The Body of Christ in America in many ways became like our sister Nation Israel, stubborn and rebellious. God still blessed us. The Body of Christ in America rebelled even more. God judged us. The Body of Christ in America repented for a season and then went right back into rebellion. Our spiritual decline was a sign that darkness had invaded our political leadership in all areas. There were many different evolutions of this. The presidency reflected the decline of the influence of the Church. The Church no longer was the influencer that it should have been. God did not leave this nation. God came and rescued us like Israel but the pattern repeated itself. You cannot repeatedly stay in rebellion against God. There comes a point when God just stops coming to the rescue and then you have to sit in that judgment.

This brings us to the 2016 Elections, no one believed President Trump would win out over Hillary Clinton. It was expected for Hillary to prevail. She was of like spirit with Obama and promised more of the same. However, God had the last say. God had a different agenda. God's agenda was to give America another opportunity to turn the tables on the antichrist spirit.

This is the proof that God is still with this nation because He could have just let us go to the dogs. Had Hillary won this nation would be in a different position in the world. This nation would be the tail and not the head. This also shows how much we as a people have changed. Losing was not an American ideal. Being content with losing would never have made it with America's greatest generation. If so the United States would have lost World War II.

President Trump is just the jolt our nation needed to turn us in a different direction. President Trump has a heart for this nation and he has respect for the original protocol that made this nation what it is today. He is working to return us to our old way of conducting business. Because of his love for this country, President Trump and his wife, Melania, restored honor to the position and hope to many Americans. The difference between President Trump and President Obama is like night and day. With President Obama there was a disdain for a core part of the people of this nation.

As one of the perks of being President, you get to decorate the White House to your own tastes and desires. Immediately after the election changes were started in the décor of the White House to bring honor and dignity back to the White House.

The White House was no longer a place where rap concerts, cocktail parties, and A-list celebrities hung out. The White House became a place of business once again. There is nothing wrong with parties but when those parties become your primary focus as a leader what are you really there to do? It is a job, not a time to relax and socialize. There have been plenty of parties at the White House over the years but the types of parties that went on served to degrade the prestige of the White House.

"First Lady Michelle Obama admitted to a crowd full of celebrities and educators that she and the president "roll pretty deep" when it comes to entertaining A-list guests. At the 2008 Inaugural Ball, Beyoncé <u>sang</u> Etta James's "At Last" for the Obamas' first dance. Guests including Jay Z, Faith Hill, Shakira, and Alicia Keys were in the crowd, <u>CNN reported</u> at the time.

In her 2012 book, The Obamas, Jodi Kantor reported a secret Halloween tea party that the Obamas held in 2009—featuring the cast of Alice in Wonderland just before their film premiered in March 2010. Johnny Depp reportedly staged the State Dining Room as the Mad Hatter's tea party, according to the book, per the New York Post. Kantor also reported that George Lucas sent over the original Chewbacca costume for the party."**xxix**

There was an overall degeneration of what is considered classy. Can you imagine the Queen of England hosting a rap concert at the palace? It is just not done. The White House was not meant to be used as a brothel, concert venue, or to host "House Parties". It is to be used to represent the very best of America. It should be seen as a place of dignity and respect, tradition and honor. When President Trump came into office this dignity was restored.

Remember what God said:

> Do you see how they are making a sham out of their king that I have chosen... they are totally disrespecting the Capitol just as they totally disrespect My throne.
> **By Pastor/Evangelist Barbara Lynch (2019)**

The American people no longer witness any of these types of events. First Lady Melania Trump took a personal interest in decorating the White House for Christmas and other holidays. It was done with class and elegance and many of the decorations were designed by her. This removed the degrading influence and anti-American Christmas scenes

that were depicted by the Obamas. The American people were bombarded with ornaments and decorations that illustrated communistic and socialistic ideologies. These ideologies were contrary to everyday American beliefs.

All things truly American have been brought back into the White House by President and Melania Trump. The celebration and appreciation of the 4th of July was a true signal that President Trump has a heart for this nation.

> "The contemporary centerpiece of Fourth of July at the "People's House" is a stunning fireworks display over the Washington Monument. On July 4, 2018, President Donald J. Trump and First Lady Melania Trump will build on this history, hosting military families and other guests on the South Lawn for music, food, and—of course—a front-row seat to fireworks over our Nation's capital."**xxx**

Did you notice how they said, "The Peoples' House"? It was not President Trumps' House. It was "The People's house".

The second area that immediately appeared was the restoration for respect for the military. President Trump has never served in the military but he acts like someone who has. He genuinely respects the brave men and women who serve this country by giving their lives in the various branches of the military. Many of our very best could not stand what was being done to the military by the Obama administration. Honorable men and women were subject to ridiculous rules and horrible abuse but that all changed under President Trump. So much so that retired S.E.A.L.S. and other military personnel made public statements that they would willingly protect President Trump or go back into the military just because of President Trump.

President Trump fixed the problems in the Veterans Administration. He was responsible for a deal with North Korea that caused North Korea to willingly return our Missing-In-Action soldiers from Korea and Vietnam. President Trump is responsible for refunding the military and giving them raises. Everything that the Obama Administration did to stop the military President Trump has reversed all of those policies and increased funding by approximately $716 billion. He has a respect for those who have served and are currently serving. The rules of engagement have been set back in our troops favor so that we can win wars and not waste our precious sons and daughters.

A remarkable accomplishment for President Trump in regards to the military is that he finally has mandated the members of NATO pay for their fair share of what they owe the United States. The NATO countries were held accountable by President Trump to boost their contribution to the alliance. President Trump is the first president to hold the NATO nations accountable. The rules in regards to fighting ISIS have been changed in favor of our troops. Their hands are no longer tied. They can use whatever force is necessary to fight this war and minimize the dangers that come from terrorism.

The third area that President Trump has worked to restore is respect for those in law enforcement. President Trump has been an advocate for the police of all types from the border patrol agents, corrections officers, and the everyday foot patrol officers who have sworn a duty to protect and serve.

> "We believe that criminals who murder police officers should immediately, with trial, get the death penalty," said Trump. "But quickly. The trial should go fast. It's gotta be fair, but it's gotta go fast."

"And there will be justice. Justice will happen. We have the people, we have the spirit, we have the mindset," said the President. "We're taking care of our law enforcement officers. And we're taking care of everybody."" *Speech by President Trump, May 2019* [xxxi]

These are the words of President Trump after speaking at the National Memorial for Corporal Ronil Singh who died during an early morning traffic stop on December 26, 2018. It's important to note that President Trump has been the leader in the fight to toughen up our laws in regards to illegal immigration. President Trump has been fought on all sides but has won the support of law enforcement everywhere. The American people know that President Trump is not just spouting rhetoric but is sincere when discussing this issue. He believes that the police should have what they need to fight crime. He has publicly blasted the leadership in Chicago for the outrageous crime rates.

"We're going to straighten it out. We're going to straighten it out fast. There's no reason for what's going on there," the president said in remarks at a law enforcement convention in Orlando. "I know the law enforcement people in Chicago, and I know how good they are. They could solve the problem if they were simply allowed to do their job and do their job properly and that's what they want to do. So Chicago, we are going to start working with you as of today. *Speech by President Trump, October 2018*"[xxxii]

Everything that President Trump does is with decency and respect. President Trump did not blame the officers for what was going wrong. President Trump blamed the leadership from the political leaders who were tying the officer's hands. He has been persistent in working with the Department of Justice to make changes to laws that have been unfair and unjust. President Trump been persistent in making changes to the laws. He signed the "First Step Act" on December 21, 2018. This law reduces the mandatory minimum sentencing requirements for Federal cases in certain circumstances for well-behaved prisoners allowing for them to serve shorter sentences.

> "The First Step Act gives nonviolent offenders the chance to reenter society as productive, law-abiding citizens. Now, states across the country are following our lead. America is a nation that believes in redemption." *Speech by President Trump, February 2019* [xxxiii]

This act is a step in the right direction and it seeks to right the wrongs that were perpetrated by the mandatory minimum sentencing which the "2010 Fair Sentencing Act" was supposed to correct. This act was supposed to reduce the disparity between crack cocaine and powder cocaine sentences at the Federal level. This law eases the 'three strikes rule" so people with three or more convictions, including for drug offenses, would automatically get 25 year sentencing instead of life for other charges. It restricts the stacking of gun charges against drug offenders to add possibly decades to prison sentences.

Isn't it funny that this law was enacted in 2010 under Obama but it never accomplished the "Social Justice" that it was intended to deliver? President Trump and Jared Kushner (His son-in-law) pushed through the red tape that kept this change from happening. What's even more hilarious is the number of people who falsely accuse President Trump of being racist. President Trump's record speaks for itself.

The fourth area that President Trump is gaining ground on is holding the media accountable for the things that the liberal media have reported erroneously over the years. President Trump is not afraid to say what he believes and hold the media accountable for the things that they have purposely reported wrongly. There has been an agenda by some in the media to impeach President Trump. It would be foolish say that only liberal media have an agenda to impeach President Trump. The truth is that there are conservative voices and liberal voices who are working against President Trump.

The Church needs to embrace this truth as well. Everything is not as fair and balanced with the media as some in the Church would like us to believe. We must start being our own voice. We must stop depending upon conservative media to get God's message out. The truth of the matter is that there are some conservative media who hate President Trump just as much the liberal media does. We have trusted those who claim to be conservative voices in the media and this needs to stop as well. We need to develop voices in the media that are not conservative or liberal but Christian. It's time that the Church takes its voice back and starts being the voice of God that is needed to speak to the darkness that is in our land. There are some conservatives who are not on President Trumps side.

> "You'll never hear me refer to [the] Russia [investigation] as a hoax or a witch hunt. I've always said Mueller should be given the time, independence and resources to complete the job he was assigned," Gowdy began. He claimed that "it is in our country's best interest for Mueller to complete the investigation as soon as possible."
> xxxiv

These are the words of former South Carolina congressman Trey Gowdy. A conservative republican voice who is now a regular on Fox News. This man by many of his actions is not for President Trump but he looks good to Christians because he attacks things that are not Christians.

> "The only national emergency is that our president is an idiot," Coulter said during the

show. She added that she was grateful Trump distanced himself from her. "Thank god he's relieved me any responsibility for what he's been doing," she said, adding "That was the biggest favor anyone could do for me."*xxxv*

These are the words of conservative commentator Ann Coulter. In no way, should our expectation be that all conservatives like President Trump. But those in the Church need to understand that just because a person has a conservative background that does not necessarily and in fact mean that they are speaking the message that we should be speaking. It does not mean that they are speaking for God. We cannot be naïve. We cannot just assume that conservative media voices are Christian voices. They are not.

Big picture thinking here. The Church must remove these types of blinders from our eyes. We have been sitting in a place of complacency thinking that conservatives are speaking for us. We have been deceived. We have been taught wrong and that scorpion is about to sting in us ways that we cannot even begin to imagine. It really is us (Christians) versus them (Non-Christians). This is why all media must be held accountable. Not just liberal media but conservative media as well. President Trump really has been battling against the principalities and powers working through the media and we need to recognize this.

The media has been working in cahoots with the democrats and republicans who have been actively fighting against him since he has been in office. The media has not hidden anything that they have done. There is a constant assault upon President Trump and his family from the moment it was announced that he won.

President Trump is not afraid to speak his mind and his heart on what he believes the media is doing. President Trump has been working to re-establish decorum and a sense of decency with his campaign against "Fake News". President Trump has used his influence to expose the untruths that are constantly being put forth by the media. President Trump has not been trying to silence the media as some reporters contend. President Trump is trying to get them to report the truth. The attacks that have come from the media upon President Trump have been never ending and relentless. He has little defense against the liberal media because at times the conservative media sides against him as well. Both sides report on what they feel he is doing wrongly.

President Trump has had to defend himself by using social media such as Twitter to tell his side of the story. President Obama was celebrated for using Twitter, President Trump is ridiculed. The leaders in media do not like that he uses Twitter. President Trump is not depending on them to tell the truth in this modern age he does quite well for himself.

President Trump and his family have been falsely accused of collaborating with the Russians so that he could cheat and win the election. After a 22-month investigation by Special Counsel Robert Mueller, President Trump and his team were found to be exonerated from all charges. There was not one single shred of evidence that he had colluded with the Russians. What is amazing about this story is how some in the media ignored all of the evidence that clearly points to President Obama and Secretary of State Hillary Clinton. This evidence shows a clear path between Obama and Clinton. As President Trump stood his ground those in the media completely ignored the truth and continued falsely accusing President Trump of colluding with the Russians.

The final area that will be addressed is how President Trump made significant impacts the area of removing regulations that have been detrimental to the growth of our economy. The Environmental Protection Agency is an agency that over the years has become a regulatory monster that grew beyond its reach. The intent of that agency had grown beyond the original scope. The regulations forced many good companies to leave the United States because they could no longer afford to pay the high fees associated with doing business here in the United States. President Trump has been working at eliminating those fees and the structures that came with them.

> "We're ending intrusive EPA regulations that kill jobs, hurt family farmers and ranchers, and raise the price of energy so quickly and so substantially," said President Trump.*xxxvi*

It's President Trump's common sense approach that has made the difference for businesses. President Trump signed executive order #13783 promoting energy independence and economic growth of this country. President further contributed by repealing the Clean Power Act. This act restricted State's authority to make choices about energy production and use within their borders. There are many other areas that President Trump has focused on but he sworn to removing government hindrances to growth in the United States.

> "We're here today for one single reason: to cut the red tape of regulation. For many decades, an ever-growing maze of regulations, rules, restrictions has cost our country trillions and trillions of dollars, millions of jobs, countless American factories, and devastated many industries. But all that has changed the day I took the oath of office, and it's changed rapidly. You've seen what's happened," said President Trump.*xxxvii*

President Trump has not been motivated by greed, or corruption. President Trump knows the protocols that started this country on the path to greatness. President

Trump knows that faith in God, strong families, hard work, and love for this country is what contributed to our success over the years. It's this return to protocol that has helped jolt our nation back into the right direction on so many levels. President Trump has taken steps to open the doors for spiritual change to take place but the Church has to join forces with God and President Trump to ensure that nothing stops what God is doing.

There are more areas that President Trump has changed and restored traditional protocols of the presidency back to their original standards. The focus on these five areas was to give you a glimpse of what is really going on behind the scenes. Everything is not as it appears with the media.

Conclusion

It's not over yet, the Battle is Just Beginning!

God's agenda is going forth. You can choose to be a part of that agenda or you can choose to stand on the sidelines and watch what happens. Now the attack is on to try to stop President Trump from finishing the journey that he started. We are more than halfway through his first term and God has promised that President Trump would win a second term. It is up to us to do our part to see that this happens.

There have been many errors in the past committed by the Church. We must not make the same mistakes. We must not assume that everything is going to be easy from this moment forward. We must not assume that conservative media is speaking the voice of God. We have a lot of work to do. We must partner with God as He wakes the Church. Whether you know it or not God is cleaning His house. There are those in whom the Spirit of God has left. Ichabod has been written across their heart and they will be found wanting of the anointing and the ability to complete the assignments that God has given them. Ichabod was the still born son of Phinehas wife. Phinehas was a priest who was corrupt. God used the death of this son to foretell what He was going to do to Israel.

We need to do our part to show President Trump that the efforts he has made and the victory he has accomplished has been noticed and appreciated by us. Our destiny as a nation is hanging in the balance because the antichrist spirit is still lurking behind the scenes eagerly moving and working with those who are held captive by principalities, powers, and spiritual hosts of wickedness in high places. We must remember that this is not just a political battle, but it is a spiritual battle that is being won by our Heavenly Father.

Our part of God's plan is not so simple. We must pray for God's agenda to continue progressing. Our prayer focus should not be from the vantage point that God cannot do it without us. It must be from the vantage point that we are agreeing with heaven that God's glory comes down to this earth. The shift from the West to the East is taking place. The focus is ever shifting and changing so that the hearts of God's first people, the Jews can be secured. We must remain grateful to God that because of their error we were given the opportunity to come and know Him. We should be in intercession for them because this truly is their time to return home. In reality they are the prodigal that the Father is eager to see return home.

We really are in for a time of rejoicing and celebrating as God brings His plan together. There will continue to be wars and rumors of wars. There will continue to be an increase in darkness. God has not revealed the rest of President Trump's story. He has already contributed much to End Time events that make up the preparations for Jesus' return to this earth. Now is the day of salvation. Now is the day when we should turn to God even more and rend our hearts. We should never place our trust in man, this includes President Trump. We should always place our trust in God. Allow the Holy Spirit to witness to you of the things that are to come.

President Trump will continue to be a sign and a wonder to My people. I have more that I am going to do through him and with him. My plans are vast and My chosen people shall return to Me with all of their hearts. I am jealous for them and all who try to hurt them will receive My wrath.

There is a works that I am asking My body to do in this season and I am asking you to not put Me in your box. I am not in your theology. I am not in your musings. I am in My word and My agenda shall go forth because I am working to bring in the sheaths.

There are many sheaths that must be brought into the storehouse. There are many who are still crying out for Me to save them. And as My body yields to Me I will give them strategies to reach them and bring them home to Me. I have many mansions with rooms to spare because I have been preparing for this day.

You shall see My son, Donald Trump slay many giants in his day. He is My servant and I can do with Him as I please. I will tread down his enemies. I will cause all to know that My hand is upon him.

I am not finished with him. I am just beginning to use him. He is a foolish thing that I am using to confound the wise inside and outside of My Church.

There will be much bloodshed in the days ahead and extreme loss of life. The days are going to be filled with tumults of all kinds but I will shine down on My son and I will radiate through him.

Many mock and ridicule him for the orange glow around about him, they do not understand that

that is My glory shining down upon him. I will never lift or relent of My promises to him. He shall always be the head and not the tail and if America heeds My voice through him then she shall prosper.

I am calling America out of her bastard state. I am calling her into My glorious light. More will be revealed in the days to come.
Prophecy: Rev. Christopher Gore – June 4, 2019

Keep watching, waiting and praying because there is more to be seen by God through President Trump. Do not be discouraged by those who say that they do not like President Trump. Stay focused on the agenda that God has been sending forth in this hour. As we have seen President Trump restore honor and respect for the military, for the police, and leaders in the political realm, we will see that transform our nation. It is inspiring new people to come on the scene and step up like never before. We all have a part to play in the restoration of honor and respect. We all can do our part to fast, pray, and intercede as God gives us the tools to help fight the forces of darkness that are seeking to have us meet the same fate that they will meet at the Judgment seat of Christ.

[11] Then I saw a great white throne and Him who sat on it, from whose face the earth and the heaven fled away. And there was found no place for them. [12] And I saw the dead, small and great, standing before [God, and books were opened. And another book was opened, which is *the Book* of Life. And the dead were judged according to their works, by the things which were written in the books. [13] The sea gave up the dead who were in it, and Death and Hades delivered up the dead who were in them. And they were judged, each one according to his works. [14] Then Death and Hades were cast into the lake of fire. This is

the second [death. **15**and anyone not found written in the Book of Life was cast into the lake of fire.

Revelation 20: 11 - 15 (NKJV)

It is not God's will that we meet this fate. It is not God's will that we allow others to meet this fate.   We must do everything in our power keep people out of Hell. We do this by living our lives before people as Jesus did. Proclaiming and living His love for all the world to see. Telling them the truth about the enemy and what his plan is for this nation and this world.

Selah

11 For it is written:
"As I live, says the Lord,
Every knee shall bow to Me,
And every tongue shall confess to God."
12 So then each of us shall give account of
himself to God.
Romans 14: 11 – 12 {NKJV}

27 And as it is appointed for men to die once, but after this the judgment, 28 so Christ was offered once to bear the sins of many. To those who eagerly wait for Him He will appear a second time, apart from sin, for salvation.
Hebrews 9: 27 – 28 {NKJV}

I realize that these truths may have shaken you to your core. I want to leave you with some hope. Not in me, but in my Savior, Jesus Christ. He died for me. He paid the price for my sins and He paid the price for yours.

Everything in this life is going to pass away. It all will be destroyed. We are destined to stand before our maker in eternity. In this life, you are presented with a choice; to accept Him as your Lord and Savior or reject Him and forever be banished into Hell with the devil and his angels. You can open your heart to Him right here right now.

When you do this you will never be alone again. His presence shall come into you and you shall be born again of the Spirit. You shall inherit eternal life because you will be an heir of His righteousness. You don't have to live in fear of the future. You can live in the love of the Father.   He is waiting for you, call on Him today.

> 13 For "whoever calls on the name of
> the Lord shall be saved." Call upon Him today
> and receive the free gift that God the Father
> has for you. **Romans 10: 13 {NKJV}**

Pray this and receive Him today

"Father, I know that I have broken your laws and my sins have separated me from you. I am truly sorry, and now I want to turn away from my past sinful life toward you. Please forgive me, and help me avoid sinning again. I believe that your son, Jesus Christ died for my sins, was resurrected from the dead, is alive, and hears my prayer. I invite Jesus to become the Lord of my life, to rule and reign in my heart from this day forward. Please send your Holy Spirit to help me obey You, and to do Your will for the rest of my life. In Jesus' name I pray, Amen."

You can contact us for help with walking out your salvation at www.lighthousechurchinc.org/contact-us/

End Notes

---

iii https://www.returnofkings.com/100445/is-hillary-clintons-entourage-involved-in-a-satanic-pedophile-ring

iv http://www.thelastamericanvagabond.com/top-news/13-essential-data-points-pizzagate-pedophilia-allegations/

v https://www.childtrends.org/news-release/new-data-on-oral-sex-among-teens

vi https://www.cbsnews.com/news/cdc-report-on-teen-oral-sex-trends-sparks-calls-for-better-education/

vii Myron Magnet https://www.city-journal.org/html/anti-cop-president-14653.html

viii Heather Mac Donald https://www.commentarymagazine.com/articles/obamas-assault-police/

ix Ibid.

x https://www.washingtonpost.com/graphics/national/obama-legacy/henry-louis-gates-jr-arrest-controversy.html?noredirect=on

xi https://algop.org/president-barack-hussein-obamas-disrespect-military-painfully-obvious/

xii Photos - https://www.somethingawful.com/news/obama-disrespect-patriot/1/

xiii https://www.nydailynews.com/news/politics/secret-service-agency-crisis-house-report-article-1.2453823

xiv https://www.cbsnews.com/news/secret-service-in-crisis-after-breaches-and-scandals-house-panel-says/

xv Transcript from Youtube video - https://oliverqueenathewatchtower.wordpress.com/2012/06/28/a-critical-look-at-the-youtube-video-obama-mocks-attacks-jesus-christ-and-the-biblevideoobama-is-not-a-christian/

[xvi] 2nd part of Transcript from Youtube video - https://oliverqueenathewatchtower.wordpress.com/2012/06/28/a-critical-look-at-the-youtube-video-obama-mocks-attacks-jesus-christ-and-the-biblevideoobama-is-not-a-christian/

[xvii] https://www.youtube.com/watch?v=QIVd7YT0oWA – video of former President Obama in Turkey 2009

[xviii] https://www.brookings.edu/blog/up-front/2011/05/20/obamas-middle-east-speech-didnt-clarify-u-s-role/

[xix] https://www.brookings.edu/blog/order-from-chaos/2016/10/19/is-a-better-world-possible-without-u-s-military-force/

[xx] https://townhall.com/columnists/chucknorris/2010/08/24/obama-muslim-missionary-part-2-n857058

[xxi] https://www.breitbart.com/national-security/2011/10/25/Report--Obamas-Muslim-Advisers-Block-Middle-Eastern-Christians-Access-to-the-White-House/

[xxii] https://wallbuilders.com/americas-biblically-hostile-u-s-president/#_edn99

[xxiii] https://www.timesofisrael.com/who-is-king-cyrus-and-why-is-netanyahu-comparing-him-to-trump/

[xxiv] https://www.cufi.org/sit-israeli-pm-netanyahu-trump-threatens-pull-us-aid-palestinians-dont-pursue-peace/

[xxv] https://www.gotquestions.org/Cyrus-Bible.html

[xxvi] https://www.mountvernon.org/library/digitalhistory/digital-encyclopedia/article/george-washington-and-religion/

[xxvii] https://www.shadesofgrace.org/2010/05/04/americas-founders-proclamations-for-fasting-and-prayer/

[xxviii] Ibid.

xxix https://www.vanityfair.com/style/2017/01/obama-white-house-parties-over-the-years

xxx https://www.whitehouse.gov/articles/look-fourth-july-white-house-past-present/

xxxi https://sanfrancisco.cbslocal.com/2019/05/15/brother-widow-slain-norcal-police-officer-ronil-singh-praise-trump-national-memorial/

xxxii https://www.politico.com/story/2018/10/08/trump-chicago-crime-doj-880976

xxxiii https://www.vox.com/future-perfect/2018/12/18/18140973/state-of-the-union-trump-first-step-act-criminal-justice-reform

xxxiv https://greatamericandaily.com/trey-gowdy-donald-trump-bad-news/

xxxv https://www.usatoday.com/story/news/politics/2019/02/16/ann-coulter-donald-trump-national-emergency-order/2890714002/

xxxvi https://www.whitehouse.gov/briefings-statements/president-donald-j-trumps-year-regulatory-reform-environmental-protection-epa/

xxxvii https://www.latimes.com/politics/la-na-pol-trump-charlottesville-transcript-20170815-story.html

Christopher A. Gore, Reverend

The Lighthouse Inc., Church.

Christopher is serving the Body of Christ as Assistant Pastor of the Lighthouse Inc., Church with his spiritual father, Barbara Lynch (Pastor/Evangelist) in Wyoming, Delaware. He and wife, Kathryn, are raising their three children Kristopher, Andrew and Kierstyn in the ways of the Lord.

He has been serving in the house of God in various capacities from early childhood. He has a deep hunger for the Word of God and this has opened a door for him to teach and minister at Lighthouse Inc., Church since 1995, Christopher was ordained by Pastor Barbara Lynch as a minister of the Gospel in 2002.

Christopher has been assisting with teaching God's word, caring for His sheep, ministering in deliverances since 1995, and instructing at the Training Center for Exorcisms. He has taught the Body of Christ in Sunday school on adult and youth level classes on various topics of the Bible. He has been a featured speaker for many services including conferences at the Lighthouse Inc., Church. He has been on the Voice of Yahweh Radio, host of Radiant Fire Radio Ministries. Christopher has composed many articles and teachings to equip the Body of Christ.

Christopher has a love for learning the deeper things of God's Word which he enjoys sharing with the Body of Christ.

He earned a Bachelor of Arts Degree in Mass Communications with a concentration in Convergence Journalism & a minor degree in Philosophy from Delaware State University.

www.ingramcontent.com/pod-product-compliance
Lightning Source LLC
Chambersburg PA
CBHW070546030426
42337CB00016B/2372